Rapture 911

10 Day Devotional

Rapture 911
10 Day Devotional

Copyright © 2019 Marsha Kuhnley
Visit the author's website at Rapture911.com

All rights reserved. No part of the non-biblical text in this publication may be reproduced, distributed, or transmitted in any form or by any means, including photocopying, recording, or other electronic or mechanical methods, without the prior written permission of the publisher, except in the case of brief quotations embodied in critical reviews and certain other noncommercial uses permitted by copyright law.

The text of the World English Bible (WEBP) is in the public domain and may be copied freely.

Published by Drezhn Publishing LLC
PO BOX 67458
Albuquerque, NM 87193-7458

Cover Design by Drezhn Publishing LLC

Print Edition - April 2020
Second Edition

ISBN 978-1-947328-32-7

All Scripture quotations are taken from the World English Bible (WEBP), a public domain translation of the Holy Bible.

RAPTURE 911

10 Day Devotional

Marsha Kuhnley

Introduction

I really enjoy reading devotionals. They've helped me make Bible reading a daily habit. On top of that they provide a truth that I can takeaway and contemplate on for the day. I've made a short devotional for you using the songs I've included in *Rapture 911: What To Do If You're Left Behind*. In *Rapture 911*, a song introduces each part of the book. I specifically chose each song because it contained biblical truths that went along with the part. I think reading and singing songs can reset and calm our hearts so we're better able to learn.

Songs are quite powerful. You know this because lyrics get stuck in your head just like they do mine. So then throughout the day we're thinking about things we've listened to. A great way to be thinking of pure and heavenly things and also learn God's word is to listen to songs that contain biblical truths. When the song enters your mind the Scripture it was based on will come to your mind as well. This is a great way to take every thought captive.

> For the weapons of our warfare are not of the flesh, but mighty before God to the throwing down of strongholds, throwing down imaginations and every high thing that is exalted against the knowledge of God and bringing every thought into captivity to the obedience of Christ. (1 Corinthians 10:4-5)

In this devotional, each day you'll read a song and a Scripture I've chosen that illustrates the biblical truths in the song. That's followed up by a brief explanation of the Scripture. Then comes the lesson and application in which I present you a key truth and a question to consider for the day. The daily reading ends with a prayer. I estimate it'll take you about five to ten minutes to read each day.

If this is your first devotional, I hope you come to love them as much as I do.

Day 1

Open My Eyes, That I May See

By Clara H. Scott. Published in 1895.[1]

Open my eyes, that I may see
glimpses of truth you have for me;
place in my hands the wonderful key
that shall unlock and set me free.
Silently now, on bended knee,
ready I wait your will to see;
open my eyes, illumine me,
Spirit divine!

Open my ears, that I may hear
voices of truth you send so clear;
and while the message sounds in my ear,
everything false will disappear.
Silently now, on bended knee,
ready I wait your will to see;
open my ears, illumine me,
Spirit divine!

Open my mouth, and let me bear
gladly the warm truth everywhere;
open my heart, and let me prepare
love with your children thus to share.
Silently now, on bended knee,
ready I wait your will to see;
open my heart, illumine me,
Spirit divine!

Scripture Reading

Paul, an apostle of Christ Jesus through the will of God, to the saints who are at Ephesus, and the faithful in Christ Jesus: Grace to you and peace from God our Father and the Lord Jesus Christ.

Blessed be the God and Father of our Lord Jesus Christ, who has blessed us with every spiritual blessing in the heavenly places in Christ, even as he chose us in him before the foundation of the world, that we would be holy and without defect before him in love, having predestined us for adoption as children through Jesus Christ to himself, according to the good pleasure of his desire, to the praise of the glory of his grace, by which he freely gave us favor in the Beloved. In him we have our redemption through his blood, the forgiveness of our trespasses, according to the riches of his grace which he made to abound toward us in all wisdom and prudence, making known to us the mystery of his will, according to his good pleasure which he purposed in him to an administration of the fullness of the times, to sum up all things in Christ, the things in the heavens and the things on the earth, in him. We were also assigned an inheritance in him, having been foreordained according to the purpose of him who does all things after the counsel of his will, to the end that we should be to the praise of his glory, we who had before hoped in Christ. In him you also, having heard the word of the truth, the Good News of your salvation—in whom, having also believed, you were sealed with the promised Holy Spirit, who is a pledge of our inheritance, to the redemption of God's own possession, to the praise of his glory.

For this cause I also, having heard of the faith in the Lord Jesus which is among you and the love which you have toward all the saints, don't cease to give thanks for you, making mention of you in my prayers, that the God of our Lord Jesus Christ, the Father of glory, may give to you a spirit of wisdom and revelation in the knowledge of him, having the eyes of your hearts enlightened, that you may know what is the hope of his calling, and what are the riches of the glory of his inheritance in the saints, and what is the exceeding greatness of his power toward us who believe, according to that working of the strength of his might which he worked in Christ when he raised him from the dead and made him to sit at his right hand in the heavenly places, far above all rule, authority, power, dominion, and every name that is named, not only in this age, but also in that which is to come. He put all things in subjection under his feet, and gave him to be head over all things for the assembly, which is his body, the fullness of him who fills all in all. (Ephesians 1)

Explanation

Paul is writing to believers, people who have put their faith in Jesus Christ. As a believer, he tells us we receive many spiritual gifts from Jesus. We're considered holy and perfect to him because he adopted us into his family of believers. We're now children of God. God displayed his grace toward us by redeeming us with the blood of his son Jesus. Grace is when we receive something we don't deserve. As sinners we deserve death. But you know that God's grace was poured out on us when Jesus was crucified for our sins. God has also revealed to believers his plan regarding Jesus. Everything on earth and in heaven will be under the authority of Jesus. This will happen at the second coming of Jesus when he sets up his kingdom on earth. What's more is that we get an inheritance because we've placed our faith in Jesus. Eternal life, a home in heaven with God, and a future reign with Jesus are all things believers inherit. In fact, Jesus gave us his Holy Spirit as a guarantee of that inheritance.

Paul prays that we have spiritual wisdom so we can fully understand how confident we should be regarding God's promises. We must open our hearts so we can see. Once we truly see, we'll understand that God's power lives within us. That same power raised Jesus from the dead.

Lesson

As a believer, you should have an enlightened heart. Do you have a confident hope that you will receive all that God has promised you? Or do you doubt God?

Application

Today, be confident in your inheritance from Jesus. When you accepted Jesus into your heart, he sealed you with his powerful Holy Spirit. Whenever you doubt, bring to mind something Jesus did or one of his qualities and let your heart be filled with hope. You know Jesus is almighty, he knows the end and the beginning, he's a counsellor, he's the creator, he's holy, he's a lion, he's the light, he overcame temptation, he's the savior, and he loves you. Now realize that you have all of those qualities and more living inside of you.

Prayer

God, thank you for everything you have blessed me with because I have placed my faith in Jesus. I pray that you help me come to know you more and more each day. As my knowledge of you grows, I pray that my confidence in your promises grows as well. Please fill my heart with your wisdom and light and give me an expectant hope for all you have promised me.

Day 2

Blessed Assurance

By Fanny Crosby. Published in 1873. [2]

Blessed assurance, Jesus is mine!
O what a foretaste of glory divine!
Heir of salvation, purchase of God,
Born of His Spirit, washed in His blood.

(Refrain:) This is my story, this is my song,
praising my Savior all the day long;
this is my story, this is my song,
praising my Savior all the day long.

Perfect submission, perfect delight!
Visions of rapture now burst on my sight;
Angels descending bring from above
Echoes of mercy, whispers of love. (Refrain)

Perfect submission, all is at rest!
I in my Savior am happy and blessed,
Watching and waiting, looking above,
Filled with His goodness, lost in His love. (Refrain)

Scripture Reading

For if we believe that Jesus died and rose again, even so God will bring with him those who have fallen asleep in Jesus. For this we tell you by the word of the Lord, that we who are alive, who are left until the coming of the Lord, will in no way precede those who have fallen asleep. For the Lord himself will descend from heaven with a shout, with the voice of the archangel and with God's trumpet. The dead in Christ will rise first, then we who are alive, who are left, will be caught up together with them in the clouds to meet the Lord in the air. So we will be with the Lord forever. Therefore comfort one another with these words.

But concerning the times and the seasons, brothers, you have no need that anything be written to you. For you yourselves know well that the day of the Lord comes like a thief in the night. For when they are saying, "Peace and safety," then sudden destruction will come on them, like birth pains on a pregnant woman. Then they will in no way escape. But you, brothers, aren't in darkness, that the day should overtake you like a thief. You are all children of light and children of the day. We don't belong to the night, nor to darkness, so then let's not sleep, as the rest do, but let's watch and be sober. For those who sleep, sleep in the night; and those who are drunk are drunk in the night. But since we belong to the day, let's be sober, putting on the breastplate of faith and love, and for a helmet, the hope of salvation. For God didn't appoint us to wrath, but to the obtaining of salvation through our Lord Jesus Christ, who died for us, that, whether we wake or sleep, we should live together with him. Therefore exhort one another, and build each other up, even as you also do. (1 Thessalonians 4:14-5:11)

Explanation

These verses describe the rapture of people who have put their faith in Jesus. The phrase "caught up" is *rapturo* in Latin and is where we get the word *rapture*. The people taken believe the gospel, that Jesus died for our sins and rose again. We learn that Jesus himself will come down from heaven and gather the believers who have already died and the believers who are still alive. They all meet in the clouds and the believers will then be with Jesus forever.

The apostle Paul further explains to us that this day will come unexpectedly. In fact, it'll come when people are living in peace and safety and thinking all is well. He likened it to a thief coming in the night. Since he's told us this in advance, we're no longer in the dark about it. So the rapture shouldn't come as a surprise to us. We're instructed to be sober or calm and clear-headed. We should be confident that God will in fact do what he says here and remove us before the time of wrath. Let's be watching expectantly for this glorious day.

Lesson

Believers are going to get raptured by Jesus one day very soon. Are you confident in God's promise and believe you'll be included? Are you looking forward to that day?

Application

Believer, rest assured if you believe with all your heart that Jesus is the son of God and that he died for your sins and rose again, you will indeed be included in the rapture when Jesus returns for his followers. Comfort your anxious soul with this promise today. Then be confidently watching for his return.

Prayer

God, thank you for this wonderful promise to gather believers together in the clouds so that we can live with you and Jesus forever. I pray that you help me not be anxious about the cares of this world. Instead, please help me be at peace and be confident that you are coming soon.

Day 3

Amazing Grace

By John Newton. Published in 1779. [3]

Amazing grace! (how sweet the sound)
That sav'd a wretch like me!
I once was lost, but now am found,
Was blind, but now I see.

'Twas grace that taught my heart to fear,
And grace my fears reliev'd;
How precious did that grace appear
The hour I first believ'd!

Thro' many dangers, toils, and snares,
I have already come;
'Tis grace hath brought me safe thus far,
And grace will lead me home.

The LORD has promis'd good to me,
His word my hope secures;
He will my shield and portion be
As long as life endures.

Yes, when this flesh and heart shall fail,
And mortal life shall cease;
I shall possess, within the veil,
A life of joy and peace.

The earth shall soon dissolve like snow,
The sun forbear to shine;
But God, who call'd me here below,
Will be for ever mine.

Scripture Reading

Being therefore justified by faith, we have peace with God through our Lord Jesus Christ; through whom we also have our access by faith into this <u>grace</u> in which we stand. We rejoice in hope of the glory of God. Not only this, but we also rejoice in our sufferings, knowing that suffering produces perseverance; and perseverance, proven character; and proven character, hope; and hope doesn't disappoint us, because God's love has been poured into our hearts through the Holy Spirit who was given to us.

For while we were yet weak, at the right time Christ died for the ungodly. For one will hardly die for a righteous man. Yet perhaps for a good person someone would even dare to die. But God commends his own love toward us, in that while we were yet sinners, Christ died for us.

Much more then, being now justified by his blood, we will be saved from God's wrath through him. For if while we were enemies, we were reconciled to God through the death of his Son, much more, being reconciled, we will be saved by his life.

Not only so, but we also rejoice in God through our Lord Jesus Christ, through whom we have now received the reconciliation. Therefore, as sin entered into the world through one man, and death through sin, so death passed to all men because all sinned. For until the law, sin was in the world; but sin is not charged when there is no law. Nevertheless death reigned from Adam until Moses, even over those whose sins weren't like Adam's disobedience, who is a foreshadowing of him who was to come.

But the free gift isn't like the trespass. For if by the trespass of the one the many died, much more did the <u>grace</u> of God and the gift by the <u>grace</u> of the one man, Jesus Christ, abound to the many. The gift is not as through one who sinned; for the judgment came by one to condemnation, but the free gift followed many trespasses to justification. For if by the trespass of the one, death reigned through the one; so much more will those who receive the abundance of <u>grace</u> and of the gift of righteousness reign in life through the one, Jesus Christ.

So then as through one trespass, all men were condemned; even so through one act of righteousness, all men were justified to life. For as through the one man's disobedience many were made sinners, even so through the obedience of the one, many will be made righteous. The law came in that the trespass might abound; but where sin abounded, <u>grace</u> abounded more exceedingly, that as sin reigned in death, even so <u>grace</u> might reign through righteousness to eternal life through Jesus Christ our Lord. (Romans 5)

Explanation

Amazing grace is the theme of Romans 5. The word *grace* occurs in these verses six times. I've underlined each occurrence for you. It's surrounded by the adjectives much more, abundance, abound, and exceedingly. It's God's grace that saves sinners. We're all sinners because Adam's sin brought sin to all of us. God gave Adam one rule: don't eat fruit from the tree of knowledge of good and evil. Adam chose to disobey God and eat from that tree anyway. Just like Adam, we all sin. God's punishment for sin is death. That's what we all deserve, a life apart from God.

However, God sent his son Jesus to die for our sins while we were all still sinners. This demonstrated how much God loves us. He doesn't wait for anyone to become perfect and holy. He knows that's impossible. Remember that grace is when we get something we don't deserve. That's what makes it amazing. It's also amazing because God's grace is far greater than Adam's sin and our own sin. We've been made right with God because we believe Jesus died for us. We've accepted God's free gift. So now we can rejoice.

Lesson

God's grace is indeed amazing and far greater than your sin. Are you trying to earn your way into heaven and make yourself right with God? Do you think you can't be forgiven because your sin is too terrible?

Application

There is absolutely nothing you can do to earn your salvation. Salvation is a gift from God that demonstrates his abundant love and grace toward us. His love conquers the most terrible of sins. It conquered every single sin that's ever been or will be committed. All God requires is that you accept his gift by placing your faith in Jesus. Today, stop striving to climb your way into heaven. Instead, rest in his grace.

Prayer

God, thank you for loving me so much that you sent Jesus to die for my sins. Your grace is truly amazing. I know that I am a sinner, and I pray that you forgive me of my sins. Help me be confident that Jesus has cleansed me of my sins and that striving to be perfect in your eyes is futile. Please fill me with your Holy Spirit, help me sin no more, and flood me with your peace.

Day 4

The Battle Hymn Of The Republic

By Julia Ward Howe. Published in 1862.[4]

Mine eyes have seen the glory of the coming of the Lord;
He is trampling out the vintage where the grapes of wrath are stored;
He hath loosed the fateful lightning of His terrible swift sword:
    His truth is marching on.

(Chorus:) Glory, Glory, hallelujah!
Glory, glory, hallelujah!
Glory, glory, hallelujah!
    His truth is marching on.

I have seen Him in the watch-fires of a hundred circling camps,
They have builded Him an altar in the evening dews and damps;
I can read His righteous sentence by the dim and flaring lamps:
    His day is marching on. (Chorus)

I have read a fiery gospel writ in burnished rows of steel:
"As ye deal with my contemners, so with you my grace shall deal";
Let the Hero, born of woman, crush the serpent with his heel,
    Since God is marching on. (Chorus)

He has sounded forth the trumpet that shall never call retreat;
He is sifting out the hearts of men before His judgment-seat;
Oh, be swift, my soul, to answer Him! Be jubilant, my feet!
    Our God is marching on. (Chorus)

In the beauty of the lilies Christ was born across the sea,
With a glory in His bosom that transfigures you and me.
As He died to make men holy, let us die to make men free,
    While God is marching on. (Chorus)

Scripture Reading

You therefore, my child, be strengthened in the grace that is in Christ Jesus. The things which you have heard from me among many witnesses, commit the same things to faithful men who will be able to teach others also. You therefore must endure hardship as a good soldier of Christ Jesus. No soldier on duty entangles himself in the affairs of life, that he may please him who enrolled him as a soldier. Also, if anyone competes in athletics, he isn't crowned unless he has competed by the rules. The farmer who labors must be the first to get a share of the crops. Consider what I say, and may the Lord give you understanding in all things.

Remember Jesus Christ, risen from the dead, of the offspring of David, according to my Good News, in which I suffer hardship to the point of chains as a criminal. But God's word isn't chained. Therefore I endure all things for the chosen ones' sake, that they also may obtain the salvation which is in Christ Jesus with eternal glory. This saying is trustworthy:

"For if we died with him, we will also live with him. If we endure, we will also reign with him. If we deny him, he also will deny us. If we are faithless, he remains faithful; for he can't deny himself."

Remind them of these things, charging them in the sight of the Lord that they don't argue about words to no profit, to the subverting of those who hear.

Give diligence to present yourself approved by God, a workman who doesn't need to be ashamed, properly handling the Word of Truth. But shun empty chatter, for it will go further in ungodliness, and those words will consume like gangrene, of whom is Hymenaeus and Philetus: men who have erred concerning the truth, saying that the resurrection is already past, and overthrowing the faith of some. However, God's firm foundation stands, having this seal: "The Lord knows those who are his," and, "Let every one who names the name of the Lord depart from unrighteousness."

Now in a large house there are not only vessels of gold and of silver, but also of wood and of clay. Some are for honor and some for dishonor. If anyone therefore purges himself from these, he will be a vessel for honor, sanctified, and suitable for the master's use, prepared for every good work.

Flee from youthful lusts; but pursue righteousness, faith, love, and peace with those who call on the Lord out of a pure heart. But refuse foolish and ignorant questionings, knowing that they generate strife. The Lord's servant must not quarrel, but be gentle toward all, able to teach, patient, in gentleness correcting those who oppose him. Perhaps God may give them repentance leading to a full knowledge of the truth, and they may recover themselves out of the devil's snare, having been taken captive by him to do his will. (2 Timothy 2)

Explanation

Believers are called to be soldiers in God's army. We're to teach the truths we've learned to others who can then pass them along to even more people. In this way, God's word isn't chained. Instead, his truth marches on.

Soldiers endure suffering, and they don't involve themselves with concerns of life. That's because they're on duty and they want to perform well for their boss. So we must do the same and work hard for God, not to earn our salvation, but to spread God's word. If we keep ourselves pure by staying away from evil, worthless and foolish talking, and uncontrolled desires then God will use us as honored soldiers. We'll be able to help lead others to the truth and rescue them from Satan's trap.

Lesson

God's soldiers spread God's word and his truth by what they say and how they live. Have you enlisted in God's army or are you just sitting on the sideline watching and commentating on the action?

Application

You can be an honored soldier for God. He delights in using us to fulfill his plans. You don't have to be a good speaker, well educated, or know every verse in the Bible. In fact, the Bible tells us God's power works best in our weakness. Today is the day for action. Do something to combat Satan's lies and deceptions and help God's word keep marching on. Consider inviting someone to church or asking someone how you can pray for them.

Prayer

God, thank you for enlisting me in your army and trusting me with helping spread your truth. I pray you fill me with the Holy Spirit and help me fulfill this calling. Guide me away from sin and into a life that speaks your truth. I know that I am weak and often get fearful of sharing my faith. Please help me be strong, bold, and speak for me like you did for Moses.

Day 5

All To Christ I Owe

By Elvina M. Hall. Published in 1882.[5]

I hear the Saviour say,
Thy strength indeed is small,
Child of weakness, watch and pray,
Find in me thine all in all.

(Chorus:) Jesus paid it all,
All to him I owe;
Sin had left a crimson stain:
He washed it white as snow.

Lord, now indeed I find
Thy power, and thine alone,
Can change the leper's spots,
And melt the heart of stone. (Chorus)

For nothing good have I
Whereby thy grace to claim—
I'll wash my garment white
In the blood of Calvary's Lamb. (Chorus)

When from my dying bed
My ransomed soul shall rise,
Then "Jesus paid it all"
Shall rend the vaulted skies. (Chorus)

And when before the throne
I stand in him complete,
I'll lay my trophies down,
All down at Jesus' feet. (Chorus)

Scripture Reading

Jesus said, "Even as the Son of Man came not to be served, but to serve, and to give his life as a ransom for many." (Matthew 20:28)

These things were done in Bethany beyond the Jordan, where John was baptizing. The next day, he saw Jesus coming to him, and said, "Behold, the Lamb of God, who takes away the sin of the world!" (John 1:28-29)

Or don't you know that your body is a temple of the Holy Spirit who is in you, whom you have from God? You are not your own, for you were bought with a price. Therefore glorify God in your body and in your spirit, which are God's. (1 Corinthians 6:19-20)

After these things I looked, and behold, a great multitude which no man could count, out of every nation and of all tribes, peoples, and languages, standing before the throne and before the Lamb, dressed in white robes, with palm branches in their hands. They cried with a loud voice, saying, "Salvation be to our God, who sits on the throne, and to the Lamb!"

All the angels were standing around the throne, the elders, and the four living creatures; and they fell on their faces before his throne, and worshiped God, saying, "Amen! Blessing, glory, wisdom, thanksgiving, honor, power, and might, be to our God forever and ever! Amen."

One of the elders answered, saying to me, "These who are arrayed in the white robes, who are they, and where did they come from?"

I told him, "My lord, you know."

He said to me, "These are those who came out of the great suffering. They washed their robes and made them white in the Lamb's blood. Therefore they are before the throne of God, and they serve him day and night in his temple. He who sits on the throne will spread his tabernacle over them. They will never be hungry or thirsty any more. The sun won't beat on them, nor any heat; for the Lamb who is in the middle of the throne shepherds them and leads them to springs of life-giving waters. And God will wipe away every tear from their eyes." (Revelation 7:9-17)

Explanation

Jesus is the Lamb of God. He sacrificed himself for our sins. He died the death that we deserve for being sinners. He did that because he loves us and wants us to partake of his glory. Jesus bought us with his own life, so we should be honoring his sacrifice with how we live.

Here we see some of the believers in heaven around the throne of God. They are praising God and Jesus and glorifying them. These are believers who put their faith in Jesus after the rapture and died during the tribulation period. They're all wearing white because their sins were purified by the blood of Jesus. They're also receiving some of the promises from God. They are not hungry, thirsty, or scorched by the sun. Nor are they crying. All of those things are no more. Instead, Jesus protects and watches over them.

Lesson

As a believer, Jesus owns your soul. He paid for it with his own life. Are you living a life that reflects how grateful you are?

Application

Today, realize that you are no longer your own. You belong to Jesus. He's washed all of your sins away. White garments that reflect your righteousness in him are waiting for you in heaven. Don't wait until you get to heaven to start behaving heavenly. You're already a citizen of heaven. Start living a life that shows the world where your true home is.

Prayer

God, thank you for washing away all of my sins with the blood of Jesus. As a sinner, I know that my life often doesn't reflect that I'm a citizen of heaven. I pray that you help me overcome the sin in my life. I want my behavior to reflect the glory that Jesus deserves.

Day 6

My Hope Is Built On Nothing Less

By Edward Mote. Published in 1834.[6]

My hope is built on nothing less
than Jesus' blood and righteousness;
I dare not trust the sweetest frame,
but wholly lean on Jesus' name.

(Refrain:) On Christ, the solid rock, I stand;
all other ground is sinking sand,
all other ground is sinking sand.

When darkness veils his lovely face,
I rest on his unchanging grace;
in ev'ry high and stormy gale
my anchor holds within the veil. (Refrain)

His oath, his covenant, his blood
support me in the whelming flood;
when all around my soul gives way,
he then is all my hope and stay. (Refrain)

When he shall come with trumpet sound,
O may I then in him be found,
dressed in his righteousness alone,
faultless to stand before the throne. (Refrain)

Scripture Reading

"Everyone therefore who hears these words of mine and does them, I will liken him to a wise man who built his house on a rock. The rain came down, the floods came, and the winds blew and beat on that house; and it didn't fall, for it was founded on the rock. Everyone who hears these words of mine and doesn't do them will be like a foolish man who built his house on the sand. The rain came down, the floods came, and the winds blew and beat on that house; and it fell—and its fall was great."

When Jesus had finished saying these things, the multitudes were astonished at his teaching. (Matthew 7:24-28)

Putting away therefore all wickedness, all deceit, hypocrisies, envies, and all evil speaking, as newborn babies, long for the pure spiritual milk, that with it you may grow, if indeed you have tasted that the Lord is gracious. Come to him, a living stone, rejected indeed by men, but chosen by God, precious. You also as living stones are built up as a spiritual house, to be a holy priesthood, to offer up spiritual sacrifices, acceptable to God through Jesus Christ. Because it is contained in Scripture,

"Behold, I lay in Zion a chief cornerstone, chosen and precious. He who believes in him will not be disappointed." For you who believe therefore is the honor, but for those who are disobedient, "The stone which the builders rejected has become the chief cornerstone," and, "a stumbling stone and a rock of offense."

For they stumble at the word, being disobedient, to which also they were appointed. But you are a chosen race, a royal priesthood, a holy nation, a people for God's own possession, that you may proclaim the excellence of him who called you out of darkness into his marvelous light. (1 Peter 2:1-9)

Explanation

In the first Scripture written by Matthew, we learn that people who listen to Jesus's teachings and obey them are wise. They have a strong foundation like a house built on rock. However, people who don't listen to or obey Jesus don't have any foundation at all, like a house built on sand. So when rains and floods come, which are like the troubles of life, the person without a foundation has a mighty fall while the person who is strong in Jesus withstands.

Peter expands on this truth by telling us that believers are living stones that God is building into his temple. Jesus is the cornerstone of this temple. He's the strong foundation we're built upon. But for people who reject Jesus, he's a stumbling stone for them. Since we're not like that, we should get rid of all bad, sinful behavior and desire the word of God. This will help us grow and do things that please God. Then our lives will reflect that God pulled us out of the darkness and into his light.

Lesson

Jesus is the strong foundation we must build upon so that we can withstand whatever comes our way. Do you desire the pure milk of God's word? Are you growing your faith?

Application

Today, make it a habit to read your Bible every single day so that you can build a strong foundation. Consider starting a one-year Bible reading plan or devotional. Use a Bible app if you need to. It'll remind you to do your daily reading and track your progress. If you're struggling with time, then start by reading just a few verses, like the verse of the day in the app. Remember that reading some is better than none. God will reward your effort by giving you a greater desire to read his word. Then you'll find you're able to devote more time to it. Pick a time of day that works best for you and stick to it. If you're already reading your Bible every day, that's great, consider starting a Bible study on a subject of interest to you.

Prayer

God, thank you for your word. I know that you wrote the Bible just for me so that I could come to know you more and more each day. I pray that you place a desire within me to devour your word. Please help me make Bible reading a daily habit.

Day 7

It Is Well With My Soul

By Horatio Spafford. Published in 1876.[7]

When peace, like a river, attendeth my way,
When sorrows like sea billows roll;
Whatever my lot, Thou hast taught me to say,
It is well, it is well with my soul.

(Refrain:) It is well (it is well),
with my soul (with my soul),
It is well, it is well with my soul.

Though Satan should buffet, though trials should come,
Let this blest assurance control,
That Christ hath regarded my helpless estate,
And hath shed His own blood for my soul. (Refrain)

My sin, oh the bliss of this glorious thought!
My sin, not in part but the whole,
Is nailed to His cross, and I bear it no more,
Praise the Lord, praise the Lord, O my soul! (Refrain)

For me, be it Christ, be it Christ hence to live:
If Jordan above me shall roll,
No pain shall be mine, for in death as in life
Thou wilt whisper Thy peace to my soul. (Refrain)

And Lord haste the day, when the faith shall be sight,
The clouds be rolled back as a scroll;
The trump shall resound, and the Lord shall descend,
Even so, it is well with my soul. (Refrain)

Scripture Reading

Therefore, my brothers, beloved and longed for, my joy and crown, stand firm in the Lord in this way, my beloved.

I exhort Euodia, and I exhort Syntyche, to think the same way in the Lord. Yes, I beg you also, true partner, help these women, for they labored with me in the Good News with Clement also, and the rest of my fellow workers, whose names are in the book of life.

Rejoice in the Lord always! Again I will say, "Rejoice!" Let your gentleness be known to all men. The Lord is at hand. In nothing be anxious, but in everything, by prayer and petition with thanksgiving, let your requests be made known to God. And the peace of God, which surpasses all understanding, will guard your hearts and your thoughts in Christ Jesus.

Finally, brothers, whatever things are true, whatever things are honorable, whatever things are just, whatever things are pure, whatever things are lovely, whatever things are of good report: if there is any virtue and if there is anything worthy of praise, think about these things. Do the things which you learned, received, heard, and saw in me, and the God of peace will be with you.

But I rejoice in the Lord greatly that now at length you have revived your thought for me; in which you did indeed take thought, but you lacked opportunity. Not that I speak because of lack, for I have learned in whatever state I am, to be content in it. I know how to be humbled, and I also know how to abound. In any and all circumstances I have learned the secret both to be filled and to be hungry, both to abound and to be in need. I can do all things through Christ who strengthens me. However you did well that you shared in my affliction. You yourselves also know, you Philippians, that in the beginning of the Good News, when I departed from Macedonia, no assembly shared with me in the matter of giving and receiving but you only. For even in Thessalonica you sent once and again to my need. Not that I seek for the gift, but I seek for the fruit that increases to your account. But I have all things and abound. I am filled, having received from Epaphroditus the things that came from you, a sweet-smelling fragrance, an acceptable and well-pleasing sacrifice to God. My God will supply every need of yours according to his riches in glory in Christ Jesus. Now to our God and Father be the glory forever and ever! Amen.

Greet every saint in Christ Jesus. The brothers who are with me greet you. All the saints greet you, especially those who are of Caesar's household.

The grace of the Lord Jesus Christ be with you all. Amen. (Philippians 4)

Explanation

Here the apostle Paul tells us that we should always be joyful. No matter our circumstance. We know that's hard because all of us tend to worry. He tells us we shouldn't worry about anything but instead we should pray about everything. When we give our worries to God, he gives us his peace in return. This peace is special because it surpasses all understanding, and it also guards our hearts and thoughts. When we're anxious and full of worry our thoughts can lead us down a dark path of despair. That's why he reiterates how important it is to think about things that are pure and lovely.

Paul learned how to be at peace and be content in every kind of circumstance. Whether he was full or hungry and whether he had a lot or none at all. That's because he knew he could do anything through Jesus who gave him strength. So we can be confident that God will indeed supply everything we need because his riches have already been given to us through Jesus.

Lesson

We're to cast all of our worries and needs upon God so we can live in peace and contentment. Have you exchanged your worries? Or are you living a life of discontent?

Application

Today, you need to unburden your heart and mind so that

everything can be well with your soul. Tell God everything you're worried about, anxious about, everything you struggle with, and all of the things you need. Of course, he already knows all of these things, but he's waiting for you to tell him so that he can take them from you. He can't fill you up with his peace if you're already full of worry. Now take a deep breath and be confident that God has everything in your life under control.

Prayer

God, thank you for taking all of my worries, troubles, and the things that weigh my heart down. Thank you for always providing for me. I pray that you give me your peace in exchange for my burdens. Help me be at ease.

Day 8

Be Thou My Vision

By Eleanor Hull. Published in 1912.[8]

Be Thou my Vision, O Lord of my heart;
Naught be all else to me, save that Thou art.
Thou my best Thought, by day or by night,
Waking or sleeping, Thy presence my light.

Be Thou my Wisdom, and Thou my true Word;
I ever with Thee and Thou with me, Lord;
Thou my great Father, I Thy true son;
Thou in me dwelling, and I with Thee one.

Be Thou my battle Shield, Sword for the fight;
Be Thou my Dignity, Thou my Delight;
Thou my soul's Shelter, Thou my high Tow'r:
Raise Thou me heav'nward, O Pow'r of my pow'r.

Riches I heed not, nor man's empty praise,
Thou mine Inheritance, now and always:
Thou and Thou only, first in my heart,
High King of Heaven, my Treasure Thou art.

High King of Heaven, my victory won,
May I reach Heaven's joys, O bright Heav'n's Sun!
Heart of my own heart, whatever befall,
Still be my Vision, O Ruler of all.

Scripture Reading

Now faith is assurance of things hoped for, proof of things not seen. For by this, the elders obtained approval. By faith we understand that the universe has been framed by the word of God, so that what is seen has not been made out of things which are visible.

By faith Abel offered to God a more excellent sacrifice than Cain, through which he had testimony given to him that he was righteous, God testifying with respect to his gifts; and through it he, being dead, still speaks.

By faith Enoch was taken away, so that he wouldn't see death, and he was not found, because God translated him. For he has had testimony given to him that before his translation he had been well pleasing to God. Without faith it is impossible to be well pleasing to him, for he who comes to God must believe that he exists, and that he is a rewarder of those who seek him.

By faith Noah, being warned about things not yet seen, moved with godly fear, prepared a ship for the saving of his house, through which he condemned the world and became heir of the righteousness which is according to faith.

By faith Abraham, when he was called, obeyed to go out to the place which he was to receive for an inheritance. He went out, not knowing where he went. By faith he lived as an alien in the land of promise, as in a land not his own, dwelling in tents with Isaac and Jacob, the heirs with him of the same promise. For he was looking for the city which has foundations, whose builder and maker is God.

By faith even Sarah herself received power to conceive, and she bore a child when she was past age, since she counted him faithful who had promised. Therefore as many as the stars of the sky in multitude, and as innumerable as the sand which is by the sea shore, were fathered by one man, and him as good as dead.

These all died in faith, not having received the promises, but having seen them and embraced them from afar, and having confessed that they were strangers and pilgrims on the earth. For those who say such things make it clear that they are seeking a country of their own. If indeed they had been thinking of that country from which they went out, they would have had enough time to return. But now they desire a better country, that is, a heavenly one. Therefore God is not ashamed of them, to be called their God, for he has prepared a city for them. (Hebrews 11:1-16)

By faith Moses, when he had grown up, refused to be called the son of Pharaoh's daughter, choosing rather to share ill treatment with God's people than to enjoy the pleasures of sin for a time, considering the reproach of Christ greater riches than the treasures of Egypt; for he looked to the reward. By faith he left Egypt, not fearing the wrath of the king; for he endured, as seeing him who is invisible. By faith he kept the Passover and the sprinkling of the blood, that the destroyer of the firstborn should not touch them. (Hebrews 11:24-28)

What more shall I say? For the time would fail me if I told of Gideon, Barak, Samson, Jephthah, David, Samuel, and the prophets— who through faith subdued kingdoms, worked out righteousness, obtained promises, stopped the mouths of lions, quenched the power of fire, escaped the edge of the sword from weakness were made strong, grew mighty in war, and caused foreign armies to flee. Women received their dead by resurrection. Others were tortured, not accepting their deliverance, that they might obtain a better resurrection. Others were tried by mocking and scourging, yes, moreover by bonds and imprisonment. They were stoned. They were sawn apart. They were tempted. They were slain with the sword. They went around in sheep skins and in goat skins; being destitute, afflicted, ill-treated—of whom the world was not worthy—wandering in deserts, mountains, caves, and the holes of the earth.

These all, having been commended for their faith, didn't receive the promise, God having provided some better thing concerning us, so that apart from us they should not be made perfect. (Hebrews 11:32-40)

Therefore let's also, seeing we are surrounded by so great a cloud of witnesses, lay aside every weight and the sin which so easily entangles us, and let's run with perseverance the race that is set before us, looking to Jesus, the author and perfecter of faith, who for the joy that was set before him endured the cross, despising its shame, and has sat down at the right hand of the throne of God.

For consider him who has endured such contradiction of sinners against himself, that you don't grow weary, fainting in your souls. (Hebrews 12:1-3)

Explanation

This is a lesson in faith. Faith is knowing the things we hope for will happen. It's being confident that things we can't see will come to pass. In all of those examples of faith each person was confidently looking forward to their promise from God. They didn't receive every promise from him, but they all died still believing. That's because they had fixed their eyes on God and heaven even though they are invisible.

We learn that we must have faith to please God. Faith first requires that we believe God exists. Then we must seek to know God and trust his promises. We must long to live in his kingdom. To live a faithful life, we must not let sin trip us up. Instead, we run our race of life with perseverance while keeping our eyes on Jesus. When we think of all that Jesus endured for us it will help us not give up. We can overcome because he overcame.

Lesson

Faith requires heaven vision. We need to see things from a heavenly point of view so that we can live every day for God and not get tired and give up. How are you showing your faith?

Application

Today, think about what you want Jesus to say about your faith when you meet him in heaven. Then write your faith verse (By faith I ...).

Prayer

God, thank you for sharing so many examples of faith in the Bible.

I pray that you help me have confidence that I will indeed receive all of the promises you have for me. I long for my future home in heaven with you and Jesus. Please fill me with your Holy Spirit and help me live a life that demonstrates my faith.

Day 9

Joy To The World

By Isaac Watts. Published in 1719.[9]

Joy to the World; the Lord is come!
Let earth receive her King!
Let ev'ry heart prepare Him room,
And Heaven and nature sing.

Joy to the earth, the Savior reigns!
Let men their songs employ;
While fields & floods, rocks, hills & plains
Repeat the sounding joy.

No more let sins and sorrows grow,
Nor thorns infest the ground;
He comes to make his blessings flow
Far as the curse is found.

He rules the world with truth and grace,
And makes the nations prove
The glories of His righteousness,
And wonders of His love.

Scripture Reading

After these things I heard something like a loud voice of a great multitude in heaven, saying, "Hallelujah! Salvation, power, and glory belong to our God; for his judgments are true and righteous. For he has judged the great prostitute who corrupted the earth with her sexual immorality, and he has avenged the blood of his servants at her hand."

A second said, "Hallelujah! Her smoke goes up forever and ever." The twenty-four elders and the four living creatures fell down and worshiped God who sits on the throne, saying, "Amen! Hallelujah!"

A voice came from the throne, saying, "Give praise to our God, all you his servants, you who fear him, the small and the great!"

I heard something like the voice of a great multitude, and like the voice of many waters, and like the voice of mighty thunders, saying, "Hallelujah! For the Lord our God, the Almighty, reigns! Let's rejoice and be exceedingly glad, and let's give the glory to him. For the wedding of the Lamb has come, and his wife has made herself ready." It was given to her that she would array herself in bright, pure, fine linen, for the fine linen is the righteous acts of the saints.

He said to me, "Write, 'Blessed are those who are invited to the wedding supper of the Lamb.' " He said to me, "These are true words of God."

I fell down before his feet to worship him. He said to me, "Look! Don't do it! I am a fellow bondservant with you and with your brothers who hold the testimony of Jesus. Worship God, for the testimony of Jesus is the Spirit of Prophecy."

I saw the heaven opened, and behold, a white horse, and he who sat on it is called Faithful and True. In righteousness he judges and makes war. His eyes are a flame of fire, and on his head are many crowns. He has names written and a name written which no one knows but he himself. He is clothed in a garment sprinkled with blood. His name is called "The Word of God." The armies which are in heaven, clothed in white, pure, fine linen, followed him on white horses. Out of his mouth proceeds a sharp, double-edged sword that with it he should strike the nations. He will rule them with an iron rod. He treads the wine press of the fierceness of the wrath of God, the Almighty. He has on his garment and on his thigh a name written, "KING OF KINGS AND LORD OF LORDS."

I saw an angel standing in the sun. He cried with a loud voice, saying to all the birds that fly in the sky, "Come! Be gathered together to the great supper of God, that you may eat the flesh of kings, the flesh of captains, the flesh of mighty men, and the flesh of horses and of those who sit on them, and the flesh of all men, both free and slave, small and great." I saw the beast, the kings of the earth, and their armies, gathered together to make war against him who sat on the horse and against his army. The beast was taken, and with him the false prophet who worked the signs in his sight, with which he deceived those who had received the mark of the beast and those who worshiped his image. These two were thrown alive into the lake of fire that burns with sulfur. The rest were killed with the sword of him who sat on the horse, the sword which came out of his mouth. So all the birds were filled with their flesh. (Revelation 19)

Explanation

Here we see some future events: the wedding supper of the Lamb and then the second coming of Jesus. Both of these events happen at the end of the tribulation period. A crowd of believers are in heaven praising God and Jesus, who is the Lamb. They're all wearing white because Jesus has made them righteous. After the wedding, heaven is opened, and Jesus rides out on a white horse to judge and make war. Jesus is wearing a robe dipped in blood because he shed his blood for us. We learn that Jesus is named Faithful and True, the Word of God, the King of all kings, and Lord of all lords. Jesus isn't alone when he leaves heaven. His army of believers follows him.

Then we see what Jesus does when he returns to earth. The "beast," who is the Antichrist, and the false prophet are both thrown into the lake of fire. That's hell. Then the entire human army that had gathered to war against Jesus is killed. Jesus kills them by speaking his word. We're reminded here that his word is indeed a sharp sword.

Lesson

Blessed are those who are invited to the wedding supper of Jesus. You don't want to be on the wrong side of Jesus's second coming. Whose side are you on?

Application

If you've placed your faith in Jesus, you're blessed and you're on the right side. You'll be at that wedding wearing white. When Jesus returns to earth, you'll be one of those believers shouting "Hallelujah." Today, think of how blessed you are here on earth and how blessed you'll be in heaven. Let it fill your heart with joy. If you haven't placed your faith in Jesus yet, then ask him into your heart today and become blessed and right with God.

Prayer

God, thank you for every single blessing you've showered upon me. Thank you for your promises like the wedding supper of the Lamb. I pray that you help me be joyful because of all you have done for me.

If you need to ask Jesus into your heart, then pray this:
Lord Jesus, I know that I'm a sinner and that I need your forgiveness so that I can live with you for eternity in heaven. Please forgive me. I believe that you are the son of God and that you died on the cross for my sins. I believe that you rose from the grave! I want to turn from my sins and trust and follow you as Lord and Savior. Please come into my heart and life. In Jesus's name, amen.

Day 10

We Believe

By Marsha Kuhnley. Published in 2019.
(To the tune of "We Three Kings")

We believe in Jesus the Christ
Coming back the day's almost nigh
Hear Him calling
Words enthralling
We look up at the sky

(Chorus:) Full of wonder at your glory
It's the start of our story
Singing, tearing
Praise and cheering
We're overwhelmed with joy

Special generation we are
Just like the wise men from afar
Watching, waiting
Anticipating
Follow you like the star (Chorus)

Waiting for you here's what we do
Bearing gifts that will honor you
Giving, knowing
Thanking, growing
It's for you we pursue (Chorus)

Introduce more people to God
This is what He wills from abroad
Bible reading
Prayer and teaching

In these He does applaud (Chorus)

Showing Christ our love we obey
Knowing one day we'll hear Him say
Outstanding, great
Let's celebrate
Enter our home and stay (Chorus)

Giving to all others we do
All we have we owe it to You
Sparing a dime
Or spending time
To Jesus it is due (Chorus)

It is coming at a quick pace
The day we see You face to face
Thankful, grateful
Ever faithful
We long for your embrace (Chorus)

Scripture Reading

Peter, an apostle of Jesus Christ, to the chosen ones who are living as foreigners in the Dispersion in Pontus, Galatia, Cappadocia, Asia, and Bithynia, according to the foreknowledge of God the Father, in sanctification of the Spirit, that you may obey Jesus Christ and be sprinkled with his blood: Grace to you and peace be multiplied.

Blessed be the God and Father of our Lord Jesus Christ, who according to his great mercy caused us to be born again to a living hope through the resurrection of Jesus Christ from the dead, to an incorruptible and undefiled inheritance that doesn't fade away, reserved in Heaven for you, who by the power of God are guarded through faith for a salvation ready to be revealed in the last time. In this you greatly <u>rejoice</u>, though now for a little while, if need be, you have been grieved in various trials, that the proof of your faith, which is more precious than gold that perishes, even though it is tested by fire, may be found to result in <u>praise</u>, <u>glory</u>, and <u>honor</u> at the revelation of Jesus Christ—whom, not having known, you love. In him, though now you don't see him, yet believing, you <u>rejoice</u> greatly with <u>joy</u> that is unspeakable and full of <u>glory</u>, receiving the result of your faith, the salvation of your souls.

Concerning this salvation, the prophets sought and searched diligently. They prophesied of the grace that would come to you, searching for who or what kind of time the Spirit of Christ which was in them pointed to when he predicted the sufferings of Christ and the <u>glories</u> that would follow them. To them it was revealed that they served not themselves, but you, in these things, which now have been announced to you through those who preached the Good News to you by the Holy Spirit sent out from heaven; which things angels desire to look into.

Therefore prepare your minds for action. Be sober, and set your hope fully on the grace that will be brought to you at the revelation of Jesus Christ—as children of obedience, not conforming yourselves according to your former lusts as in your ignorance, but just as he who called you is holy, you yourselves also be holy in all of your behavior, because it is written, "You shall be holy, for I am holy."

If you call on him as Father, who without respect of persons judges according to each man's work, pass the time of your living as foreigners here in reverent fear, knowing that you were redeemed, not with corruptible things like silver or gold, from the useless way of life handed down from your fathers, but with precious blood, as of a lamb without blemish or spot, the blood of Christ, who was foreknown indeed before the foundation of the world, but was revealed in this last age for your sake, who through him are believers in God, who raised him from the dead and gave him <u>glory</u>, so that your faith and hope might be in God.

Seeing you have purified your souls in your obedience to the truth through the Spirit in sincere brotherly affection, love one another from the heart fervently, having been born again, not of corruptible seed, but of incorruptible, through the word of God, which lives and remains forever. For,

"All flesh is like grass, and all of man's <u>glory</u> like the flower in the grass. The grass withers, and its flower falls; but the Lord's word endures forever."

This is the word of Good News which was preached to you. (1 Peter 1)

Explanation

Peter is writing to believers. He's speaking about the forthcoming revelation of Jesus to the world. I underlined some of the descriptive words he uses that reveal a theme: *glory, honor, praise,* and *joy*. It's a celebration!

He tells us we've been washed by the blood of Jesus and made holy. In fact, we've been born again because we've placed our faith in Jesus. We know that Jesus died for our sins and rose from the grave. We have an incorruptible and perfect inheritance reserved for us in heaven, eternal life. Our salvation is so wonderful that the prophets of old wanted to understand it better and even the angels are intrigued. So we have reason to greatly celebrate.

Even though we face many trials ahead, those trials demonstrate our faith. Our faith is more precious than gold, and it's being tested in the same way fire purifies gold. When we endure, we bring glory to Jesus. We must exercise self-control and live a holy life. We're instructed to look forward to seeing Jesus revealed to the world. When he comes, he's going to reward each of us for the work we've done for him.

Lesson

We have good reason to celebrate! We believe in Jesus, we're guaranteed eternal life, and his glory will soon be revealed to everyone. Are you ready for the party?

Application

Today, don't think about all the things you hope to accomplish here on earth before Jesus comes back. Instead, look forward to all the incorruptible things you'll get when Jesus is revealed. A brand-new body, eternal life, treasure in heaven, and a home with Jesus. Look forward to the party!

Prayer

God, thank you for promising Jesus's return and for giving me so many reasons to celebrate. I pray that you help me endure the trials that are testing my faith. I want to be holy because you are holy. I don't want to be ashamed of my behavior when Jesus returns. Help me look forward to seeing Him face to face.

Thanks for reading this devotional. If you'd like to show your support for my work, please leave a review wherever you purchased this book. It's free to do, and it'll only take you a minute to write a quick sentence expressing your thoughts about the book. Your review is very important to independent, self-published authors like me. Internet and online bookstore algorithms favor books with reviews. They display in search results and at the top of search results more often than books without reviews. I even need a minimum number of reviews before I can purchase certain advertising. So, your review will help more people find this book. That will in turn help me sell more books, which means I can keep writing books for you. Go to rapture911.com/reviews if you need a link to where you can leave a review.

Thanks for your support!

Marsha

Read
Rapture 911:
What To Do If You're Left Behind

The End of the World is coming...

...but it's not what Hollywood portrays.

Are you uncertain about what God has in store for humanity? Do you fear for the salvation of your family and friends?

It could happen any minute.

The Rapture.
Will you be Left Behind to survive the Apocalypse? You can join the millions who will be saved.

Do you already believe? Then you can help those who are Left Behind. *Rapture 911: What To Do If You're Left Behind* is your all-in-one resource to survive the Tribulation and prepare for Jesus's Second Coming.

Inside this book is the following:
- Easy-to-understand Biblical analysis.
- Theological overview of forthcoming events surrounding the End Times.
- Why millions of people will disappear and what those Left Behind can do to be saved.
- The truth behind fake news and deceptions surfacing today that will be prominent after the Rapture.
- Examples of prophecies fulfilled that prove God's Word is trustworthy.
- Coping mechanisms from Biblical heroes to better handle shame, grief, and fear.
- A checklist of preparations, a handy glossary, and much, much more!

You'll love this handbook for navigating the Last Days because you want to live in Heaven and you care about saving your loved one's souls.

Get it now.

Books By Marsha Kuhnley

Rapture 911 Series
*Rapture 911: What To Do If You're Left Behind
Rapture 911: What To Do If You're Left Behind (Pocket Edition)
Rapture 911: 10 Day Devotional
Rapture 911: Prophecy Reference Bible

End Times Armor Series
The Election Omen: Your Vote Matters
The Election Omen: 10 Day Devotional

Other Works
Seeing The Light In Dark Times: 10 Day Devotional

Visit Marsha's website to find these books
rapture911.com

* - Also available as an audiobook

About The Author

Marsha Kuhnley is an American author of Christian non-fiction books. She has a passion for Bible prophecy, finance, and economics. She received her MBA in Finance and BA in Economics from the University of New Mexico. Prior to becoming an author, she enjoyed a career at Intel Corporation. She uses her education and career experience to take complex Biblical information and present it in easily understandable concepts. You'll benefit from over a decade of her research and study of the Bible, Bible prophecy, and Rapture theology. She lives in Albuquerque, NM with her husband where they attend Calvary Church.

Connect With Marsha

rapture911.com/connect

Endnotes

1 "Open My Eyes, That I May See," Hymnary.org, https://hymnary.org/text/open_my_eyes_that_i_may_see, Accessed September 7, 2019.

2 "Blessed Assurance," Hymnary.org, https://hymnary.org/text/blessed_assurance_jesus_is_mine, Accessed September 7, 2019.

3 John Newton and William Cowper, Olney Hymns: In Three Books, (London, 1779), 53-54, https://www.loc.gov/resource/rbc0001.2006pre79197/, accessed September 7, 2019.

"Amazing Grace," Wikipedia, https://en.wikipedia.org/wiki/Amazing_Grace, accessed September 7, 2019.

"Amazing Grace! (how sweet the sound)," Hymnary.org, https://hymnary.org/text/amazing_grace_how_sweet_the_sound, Accessed September 7, 2019.

4 "Battle Hymn Of The Republic," Wikipedia, https://en.wikipedia.org/wiki/Battle_Hymn_of_the_Republic, accessed September 7, 2019.

"Battle Hymn Of The Republic," Hymnary.org, https://hymnary.org/text/mine_eyes_have_seen_the_glory, Accessed September 7, 2019.

5 "Jesus Paid It All," Hymnary.org, https://hymnary.org/text/i_hear_the_savior_say_thy_strength_indee, Accessed September 7, 2019.

J.J. Little & Co., Hymns And Tunes, (New York, NY: J.J. Little & Co., 1882), 840, https://books.google.com/books?id=Y1AXAAAAYAAJ&dq, accessed September 7, 2019.

6 "My Hope Is Built On Nothing Less," Hymnary.org, https://hymnary.org/text/my_hope_is_built_on_nothing_less, Accessed September 7, 2019.

7 "Horatio Spafford," Wikipedia, https://en.wikipedia.org/wiki/Horatio_Spafford, accessed September 7, 2019.

"It Is Well With My Soul," Wikipedia, https://en.wikipedia.org/wiki/It_Is_Well_with_My_Soul, accessed September 7, 2019.

"When Peace, Like A River," Hymnary.org, https://hymnary.org/text/when_peace_like_a_river_attendeth_my_way, Accessed September 7, 2019.

8 "Be Thou My Vision," Wikipedia, https://en.wikipedia.org/wiki/Be_Thou_My_Vision, accessed September 7, 2019.

"Be Thou My Vision," Hymnary.org, https://hymnary.org/text/be_thou_my_vision_o_lord_of_my_heart, Accessed September 7, 2019.

9 "Joy to the World," Wikipedia, https://en.wikipedia.org/wiki/Joy_to_the_World, accessed September 7, 2019.

"Joy To The World! The Lord Is Come!," Hymnary.org, https://hymnary.org/text/joy_to_the_world_the_lord_is_come, Accessed September 7, 2019.

www.ingramcontent.com/pod-product-compliance
Lightning Source LLC
Chambersburg PA
CBHW052124110526
44592CB00013B/1744